Fight to Get YOU Back
He Made Me Better Than This

Dr. Monica Belcher

WriteHouse Publishing
Washington, DC

ISBN: 0692398120
ISBN-13: 978-0692398128

DEDICATION

To the memory of my incredible father, DeWitt Talmadge Belcher who manifested his love for God through his love for his family.

CONTENTS

ABOUT THE AUTHOR

Having been reared in a home accustomed to serving in ministry, from birth Monica Belcher was taught to honor God with her heart and in service whenever called on. Monica is now centered in God's divine purpose as the COO of Build Forward Missions; an effective non-profit ministry touching lives locally and globally. This anointed messenger flows in a gentle power with a testimony that Christ will apply healing balm to all manner of relational sickness and disease and He will massage your aching heart until the pain completely disappears. **Psalm 147:3, *"He heals the brokenhearted and binds up their wounds."***

Educated in the public schools of the District of Columbia and Howard University; Monica received her Doctorate as a graduate of Faith Bible College & Universities. Monica's commitment to serving is evidenced through untiring efforts to provide programs, education and training with an emphasis on practical application.

The proud parent of two, Toniah and Christopher. Loving 'Granby' to four beautiful grandchildren: Jamel, Michelle, Christopher Jr. and Aaron.

He Made Me Better Than This...

will challenge you and uncover many issues that have become taboo to discuss especially in our churches. You'll be motivated toward a more rich and satisfying life in Christ Jesus. In this offering God's voice is clear, powerful and strengthening. Seek Him, and you will find Him! Hear Him and your soul shall live!

**The complexities of our lives require
the grace and mercy of our God.**

Forward

It was a Tuesday morning and seemed like just another weekday. Yet, there was an overwhelming unrest in my spirit, the kind of unrest that makes you pray and stay on high alert until you feel a definitive release from the Holy Spirit. I tried to go on as usual but there was a critical press to pray with fervency. Somewhere around 10:30 am, I clearly heard the Lord say, *"Go get Monica, right now!"* I knew without a doubt this was the Lord. I let my director know I would be returning but there was an urgent matter I needed to attend to.

Amazingly, the Lord had worked it out that our jobs were a little less than two miles apart. I jumped in a cab, went into her building, called upstairs and asked her to meet me in the lobby. The fact she didn't ask why should have been a heads up for me, that's just how Monica was. She stood there saying nothing and when I looked into her empty eyes the Holy Spirit let me know she was seconds away from a complete mental collapse due to the incredible degree of stress she had been under. We'd been in spiritual warfare fighting an intensely alarming, and grueling battle for a long, long time. In that one moment I saw her agony, her anguish, her desperation and her silent cry for help; help only the Lord God Himself could give. We were at a major impasse, 'the make you or break you' point. My heart hurt to see Monica like this but I could not allow my emotions to get in the way, *I was on assignment.* I embraced her…tightly. I had no words, no answers but I had the Lord guiding me every single step of the way.

We left the building and walked towards Georgetown.

Neither of us spoke for a brief period but that didn't matter, I knew the enemy had been defeated because Monica was not left uncovered. I'm grateful for the disciplines of prayer; I've learned to just obey God and let Him take care of the results. I waited until Monica could talk and when she finally did along with her words came the flood of reality she had not allowed herself to feel up to that moment. Here's the thing though, there was a supernatural dichotomy going on – for the first time *she made herself experience the devastation of everything* she was going through but at the same time *I witnessed the birth of a warrior.* You see before that moment, Monica had taken a very passive; there is nothing I can do, already beaten approach. It's in these type of life-changing moments the devil seems to forget when he pushes God's people too far we often fight ourselves right into His perfect will. I went back to work assured of two things: 1) **God was in full control**; and 2) God could now escalate the battle because Monica was yielded to whatever He was doing in her life.

The Bible says**, "And they overcame him by the blood of the Lamb, and the word of their testimony; and they loved not their lives unto the death."** Get ready to be ministered to by a victorious overcomer who has been commissioned by God to share her testimony. The result: Healing fruit that only comes from abandoning all for the cause of Christ. Monica let go of resistance, refused to be removed from her circumstances, restrained from trying to talk God out of His plan and rejected the convenience of turning back when her whole world was turned upside down. Jesus said, *"If any man will come after me, let him deny himself, and take up his cross, and follow me."* Monica did just that, she has been the first partaker; she has lived, breathed, received deliverance and healing strength through every word written in this book. Take heart and rejoice, the precious oil of God's anointing will flow fresh for you and those you love as you read, *"He Made Me Better Than This."*

by Dr. Charlene Nelson
Author of *'Praisentations: Presenting PRAISE that's Pleasing to GOD'* and *'N.I.C.H.E. – Now I Can Have Everything'*

He Made Me Better Than This

Prologue

The story we're going to examine in our lesson is one you may be familiar with but probably had not seen or considered it in the way we're going to look at it.

Our lesson is filled with many causal agents that lend themselves to abuse and poor or low self-esteem, which is what we're focusing on. Although we hear these terms quite often and with great frequency, society does not necessarily want to label every dysfunction as abuse and low self-esteem, or its close cousin. But the fact is now we have identified what they are, we have come to the realization that these conditions have been prevalent in our communities, our churches, and our families for eons. We have just ignored them or we recognized them and chose not to deal with them. So many people have suffered greatly as a result of these conditions. Abuse didn't just start in the Catholic Church, and it's not limited to the Catholic Church by any means nor is it solely of a sexual nature. It is quite prevalent in many faiths/denominations as well, and in almost every facet of public and private life. We see abuse in child day care facilities, coach and athlete relationships, with stepdad and daughter, son and father, teacher and student, boss and employee, etc, etc, etc. We are now just coming to the knowledge of what had been going on for so very long and how so many lives have been permanently altered as a result of the abuse.

The headlines were filled in the fall of 2002 with articles about the sniper in the Washington DC metropolitan area. With great dismay we learned the convicted teenager involved with the killings suffered abuse as a child and had a very poor sense of self worth. He was shuttled from pillow to post and had no security in his young life. Those conditions made it very easy for the enemy to prey upon his need to belong and have the stability he felt he found, to a degree, from his accomplice. Textbook cases of mass murders list abuse and low self-esteem among the variables and characteristics often seen in those who are executioners of deadly criminal acts. Regrettably, we're beginning to see these acts on a regular basis to the point that acts which once would stop regular programming to cover are now a mere 2 line cover on our local news.

So, as we see the light we must walk therein. As we understand these disorders, come to the knowledge of the truth, we grow and make changes so we won't suffer the same mistakes continually nor subject future generations.

Solomon tells us in Ecclesiastes 1:9c, *"There is **nothing new** under the sun."* And he is absolutely correct. There is nothing new under the sun. There have been problems with people relating to one another every since there have been people. The first family suffered murder because one brother was jealous of the other. Adam projected his guilt upon Eve because he was too weak to say no; as a result they both lost their fellowship with the almighty God because they allowed themselves to be influenced wrongly by another. If life and mankind starts out that way, it's not difficult to see how we've evolved to a society of carelessness and harm inflicting our wants and demands on others without caring about whom they are and the individuality of their God given rights. Biblical society is a foreshadowing of present day society wherein a person is totally disregarded so the wants and desires of another can be met, at a very great cost. That cost???...is losing one's self and often not having the opportunity to get "You" back.

Our need is urgent, so let us begin.

He Made Me Better Than This

1} NOTHING NEW UNDER THE SUN

Although times have changed since that of biblical days, times really have *not* changed. Some forms of abuse are so blatant a blind man is able to see it. But then, there are those cases where people have been able to disguise it and present it as an expression of love and care while completely destroying the recipient. People who perpetrate abuse want others, outsiders, to believe the victim is over-reacting and there is nothing wrong in the camp, oh, but God says differently.

WHAT EXACTLY IS ABUSE?

Let's get a working definition of abuse. What is it? Abuse is to use wrongly or improperly; to treat in a harmful, damaging way; or mistreatment of some kind. Although that definition may be too simplistic to you, it is nevertheless what it is. Any act that alters or takes away from the natural rights of an individual without their permission or agreement and sometimes with their agreement is abuse.

Self-esteem is self-respect; a favorable opinion of oneself. Conversely, low self-esteem therefore is a low degree or level of respect for you and an unfavorable opinion of oneself. Low self-esteem is associated with and can be a result of abuse; how others treat you.

As we have already mentioned, abuse is not always physical, it's often mental, psychological and is hard to recognize because the wounds and bruises are not visible. And, men and women who have long since left the abuse behind often still find themselves wrestling, years later, with the effects of what traumatized their lives for so long.

Abuse and low self-esteem in relationships is most often assumed to be associated romantically between the sexes. But I must caution you, it's multifaceted, not limited to romance and can be seen in the family, in the church, in the workplace. It can be physical, spiritual, emotional and mental or some of all these. And there is often a great deal of overlapping.

Sadly enough, you can become so use to abuse or blinded by it that it often seems easier to just continue to be a part of it as opposed to seeking help to save yourself from it. Unfortunately, there are instances wherein that way of life can seem normal because you've never been exposed to anything else. God help us. The enemy has made some lives a living hell. But God does not want you to continue to allow the enemy to determine the direction your life takes. God is a healer and a deliverer and there is no situation so great He can't turn it around. He is all-powerful and He will help you! It takes strength and courage to change adversity that has settled in with the passing of so much time. But, there is nothing too hard for God!

WOMEN: THE WEAKER SEX?

In a society like that of biblical times, the mistreatment of women was commonplace and was not thought as such; though not all viewed it in that light. Women were viewed as property, right along with land and livestock and they were expected to be just as productive. A woman knew what was expected of her and anything outside of keeping the home and having children was not something openly expressed. It's not that women didn't have dreams and thoughts about a life that offered them more; it's more so they didn't talk about those dreams. Even though we've come a long way in today's society with regard to women's worth, much attention still needs to be given to our plight as the defined "weaker of the two sexes." That term, "weaker of the two sexes" has been exploited for so long to mean 'less than' when in actuality it really means *physically* we are weaker. With few exceptions, the physical make-up of a woman is such that she is not as strong as a man because her body simply is not built that way; God knew exactly what He was doing. But there certainly is not a gene in the woman's physiology that dictates her intellect is less than that of a man, assuming in this equation he is the superior of the two beings. Life in American today speaks to the equality of the sexes. We have women who are CEO's of major corporations, senators, doctors, head of families, diplomats, educators, owners of radio/TV conglomerates, pastors, and women find themselves in arenas that were once limited to "men only." So, the term "weaker of the two sexes" has through the years proven to be a misnomer.

2} CHILD ABUSE

LABAN USED LEAH AND EXPECTED HER TO BE QUIET ABOUT IT

Genesis 29 starting with verse 20 in the Living Bible reads, *"So Jacob spent the next seven years working to pay for Rachel. But they seem to him but a few days, he was so much in love. Finally the time came for him to marry her."* Verses 23-26: *"Afterwards, that night, when it was dark, Laban took Leah to Jacob and he slept with her. But in the morning, it was Leah! What sort of trick is this? It's not our custom to marry off a younger daughter ahead of her sister, Laban replied smoothly."*

If you know the story you know Jacob, the nephew of Laban comes along in his travels, identifies himself as Rebekah's son, is attracted by the beautiful Rachel, Laban's youngest daughter and helps her with the sheep. He winds up working and staying with Laban for a month. As payment for his labor, Laban tells Jacob to ask what he will of him. Jacob asks for Rachel's hand in marriage. Laban agrees, with the condition that Jacob works seven years before he can have Rachel as his wife. Jacob readily agrees.

Where we look in on the scripture above the seven years have been worked, they've had the bridal celebration party and Jacob goes to bed overjoyed and expecting Rachel. Now, here in our story we have the promise of a daughter's hand in marriage, Rachel, and the deceit and trickery of her father, Laban. He denies Rachel her husband, and forces Leah, the unrequited daughter/sister as wife to an unsuspecting Jacob.

Jacob's rage is understandable and Laban has created the situation where he has ushered his daughter Leah into a relationship, a marriage where she is unloved, unwanted, and rejected. Now, by our definition of abuse, i.e., to be used wrongly or improperly, there are several observations gleaned from this text.

Laban's intentions were not honest from the beginning as evidenced by his response to Jacob in verse 26: *"It's not our custom to marry off a younger daughter ahead of her sister."* The argument could very easily be made that Jacob got his just reward in that he was tricked by Laban to marry Leah. After all, Jacob was reaping the seeds of deceit he had already sown. Remember how he obtained the blessing of the birthright from his father Isaac? He used the opportunity of his brother, Esau suffering from extreme hunger to take away the pre-determined blessing from Esau. Then, he went along with the scheme his mother concocted to dress in such a way that his father, in failing health and failing eye sight would not be able to differentiate between Jacob and his brother Esau. So God allowed Laban, who was already predisposed to lying and trickery, to serve as the vehicle by which Jacob received the fair return of that which he had planted. Jacob's name means supplanter, "taking the place of another." While it is God told Rebekah, Jacob and Esau's mother in a dream Esau would serve his brother Jacob, she felt God needed their help to make it happen. She wanted to help God out like her mother-in-law Sarah when she felt she was too old to bear the son God had promised her and Abraham. As demonstrated in the earliest of God's people, we get impatient waiting for God to do what He has told us He would do and we try to help Him; always making matters worse. The timing of the Lord is perfect and whenever we alter the sequence of events, we run the risk of either completely changing the alignment of what needs to happen in God's ordained order, or even more detrimental, forfeiting completely what He had designed.

So, Laban set Jacob up. When Laban made the contract, *"Work seven years and you can have her...*" he knew he was not going to allow it to happen that way. Laban was getting a lot of free labor out of Jacob. And he was being blessed by having Jacob around. It appeared everything Jacob was associated with was blessed; consequently, Laban was blessed too. And if Jacob loved Rachel as much as it appeared he did, Laban's thought could have been, marry him off to the oldest and he will stay longer to get the youngest. At any rate, Laban was dealing underhandedly with Jacob from the beginning.

Vital insights to this story:

- According to custom, when a couple was betrothed, after the man got the father's permission to marry his daughter, which Jacob did, then there would be a public announcement. Jacob and Rachel didn't get the public announcement and Laban made sure he never called the bride-to-be by name so he could not be held liable as to entering into a contract and then reneging.

- But too, Jacob was not without fault either in the making of the contract. He knew it was customary to marry the oldest daughter first but he thought his generous offer, in terms of the dowry, would bribe Laban into giving him what he wanted. The average maximum bridal price was 50 shekels. One year wage was 12 shekels, one shekel per month. Jacob's offer of 84 shekels was 34 shekels more than what would be expected. Knowing how materialistic Laban was, Jacob thought he could bribe him into ignoring what the marriage custom was. Again Jacob tries to turn the tables, as it were, to benefit himself. In this case, things would not turn out as he had supposed.

Parents can and do abuse their God-given authority

Leah was not oblivious to everything that was happening; she had the knowledge Rachel was expecting to marry Jacob. And yet, Laban came to her and told her to pretend she was the expected bride of Jacob. She was to keep quiet about it and pretend to be someone she wasn't. What Laban did was abusive in that he exerted power and control over both his daughters, which caused very negative consequences in their lives for days and years to come. Laban asked Leah to lie about who she was and to pretend to be someone she wasn't just as Abraham had done when he told Sarah to pretend to be his sister and not his wife. Laban was a great father for instilling character and values in his children, huh? Anything but!

It's important for me to highlight here Jacob was not always the trickster or liar he had become. At some point there was a purity and innocence about him, as God had created him to be. At what point did he change? When was it he ceased to be who God created him to be? I am sure there were many factors involved in the denigration of 'God's Jacob.' When mother Rebekah came to him with the scheme to deceive his father, because of who God had made Jacob to be, there had to be something inside him crying out, "This is not right." Why wasn't he strong enough to say, "Mother, I love you but this is deceitful and I can't be a part of what you're trying to do." Is this the point the seed of deception was planted in him? How great a role did his mother play in contaminating his character and infecting his integrity? In **Genesis 27:8** and verses **12-13** Rebekah says to Jacob, *"Now therefore, my son, obey my voice according to that which I command thee."* Jacob said with conviction, *"My father peradventure will feel me, and I shall seem to him as a deceiver; and I shall bring a curse upon me, and not a blessing. And his mother said unto him, upon me be thy curse, my son; only obey my voice and go fetch me them."* God made Jacob one person but he allowed his mother's influence to help make him someone else.

God-directed reflection will begin the process of healing

Reflection may cause you to look back and try to pinpoint where exactly it was you started seeing the hints of change taking place in your life.

As a child I knew God. My parents brought me up in the church and I knew who God was. I remember having a life of prayer and fasting. I remember for an entire school year fasting through my lunch period as I petitioned God for the healing of my loved one. I remember the hand of the Lord being on me when I was as young as eight years old but also I remember at points when what God wanted and what my mother wanted did not agree and it was more important to me to have her approval than it was to have the approval of God. I think I thought God and mother would get together and work out what they thought was best for me; you know…the two of them would come to some sort of agreement. It was at this very point I now see I was refusing to take responsibility for my own life. *I wanted others to make decisions for me* and was quite comfortable allowing them to do just that. I cry as I look back because I painfully see how I once knew Him in a real and tangible way and where our roads separated. And I see how long and painful the road has been in me getting back to the person He created me to be. I've always seen myself as the victim but I've had to come to grips with the fact I collaborated with the enemy. It wasn't all the other person's doing. I allowed these things to take place to a great degree. I didn't fight for my survival; I went right along with the program.

My need to have the approval of others didn't end there. I spent 20 years in a marriage where I allowed myself to be manipulated beyond measure for the appearance of peace and the appearance of happiness all for the sake of family. What I wanted was never important to me; it was always what the other person wanted. God was neither being honored nor glorified. But He loved me enough not to leave me there. He loved me enough to rescue me from me and for you.

There have been many tearful days in my life because getting back to me was not and is not easy. The enemy isn't sitting idly by conceding defeat as I waltz myself back to God's design for me. The attacks continue, and the games are still being played because he still thinks he can win. But God is there constantly reminding me Satan is a defeated foe and God is holding me tight; healing me and moving me forward.

Becoming dysfunctional is not a mere cliché

God had plans for Jacob and his deviant behavior caused him to delay what was intended for him. God had already intended for Jacob to be the father of the twelve tribes of Israel. Do you think that mattered to Satan? No, why should it? He's the enemy and he doesn't care what he uses to move you out of place with God. His goal is simple; keep her / keep him from reaching their destiny. He expends a whole lot of energy to make sure you don't get there. We have to expend a whole lot of focus to make sure we do. Psalm 121:5-8 reminds us, *"The Lord is thy keeper; the Lord is thy shade upon the right hand. The sun shall not smite thee by day, nor the moon by night. The Lord shall preserve thy going out and thy coming in from this time forth, and even for evermore."*

There were issues in Laban's family but Jacob's family gives a whole new meaning to a dysfunctional family. Remember, we just talked about the deception perpetrated by Jacob and his mother Rebekah. Far beyond that there is conflict that goes deeper to the core. Scripture refers to Esau as Isaac's son and to Jacob as Rebekah's son. Author David Esau in, The Dysfunctional Biblical Family talks about the "emotional triangle" when two people become uncomfortable with each other, they focus on a third person as a way of stabilizing their relationship. Meaning there is conflict between Isaac and Rebekah with their fight over which son should receive the birthright. Instead of keeping this among themselves, they bring their sons into the conflict; Rebekah favoring Jacob, Isaac favoring Esau. Isaac is viewed as the common enemy. With the deception of Isaac by Jacob and with fear of Esau rage, Jacob runs. Issues are unresolved with him and instead of settling things at home he leaves and gets enthralled in another conflict headed by his uncle Laban, the master of deception. Jacob then stands idly by and does nothing about the ensuing conflict between Rachel and Leah even after having experienced what he had in relationship with his own brother.

FAMILY SECRETS

How often are injustices committed in our families? People suffer wrongful acts and are expected to keep silent about them. With serious conviction and a promise of impending punishment you're told things like, "What goes on in your family stays in your family. You don't air our dirty laundry in public." To some extent not talking about family matters is made to appear as though it's an act of nobility and honor; as a family we're strong and we handle our personal matters without needing the help of others. *That's pride in disguise*. But not only are you not allowed to discuss it *outside* of the family, so very often there is the spoken and unspoken rule of 'the family way of doing things' meaning you are not even allowed to talk about real issues with members in your immediate family. Secrets are kept, without ever seeking a discussion or resolve between fathers and sons, mothers and daughters, daughters and fathers, mothers and sons, and sibling's one to another. So, you suffer in silence. Your rights have been taken away from you. There is no freedom of speech; there is no speech. You cry inside because you need to be heard. You've become a party to deceit, you've become a liar, all against your will and you're not to say anything about it to anyone or else.

There are people too numerous to count who have held on to dark family secrets that have totally altered who they would have been had they not been apart of the silence. Sometimes that 'abuse of silence' can be the seed to infestations of guilt, anger, hate, resentment, loss of self-worth, anxiety, fear and the list goes on. The root of so much malcontent and malfunction in an individual's life can so often be traced back to family situations trapped behind four walls and closed doors. The abuse is so easily perpetrated because in families you have intimate, co-dependent relationships and the threat of loosing the perceived family bond helps keep the victim silent. There are too many children in society who have been strapped with the burden of silence that has snatched from them their innocence, their purity, their youth, their trust, and their peace; sidetracking them from what God meant for them in the institution of family.

In co-dependent adult relationships you have the one person who feels they cannot survive or make it in life without the help of the other person. Co-dependency causes one to often feel that the other person defines them and all of their support comes from them. That's not healthy, that's a handicap. That means you are at a disadvantage and it makes achievement in any aspect of life seem overwhelmingly difficult. God didn't create you to be at a disadvantage, at the mercy or the behest of someone else. He didn't create you for life dependency on anyone except Himself. Life has somehow put that burden on you, but God is always nigh to restore you back to the "You" He created you to be.

FATHERS: PRIESTS AND PROTECTORS

Let us not forget about Laban and the role he is responsible for in the home. As the man, not only is he the provider for his family, he is also the protector and the priest. He is responsible for the physical growth, emotional growth, and spiritual growth of his family. As father, he is the first exposure a child is expected to have, in this case his daughter, to a healthy male/female relationship.

In the home, the introduction to and knowledge of God comes from the priest. How many young people have decided against God and a relationship with Christ because the interaction with their father has been so offensive, abusive and unprotected? They somehow draw a correlation between what they have experienced with their father and being in relationship with the Lord. We pray, "Our Father," and yet, the only father they have known has failed to nourish, provide, comfort, teach, and love them. The father is the head of the home as Christ is the head of the church and sadly enough there have been too many that have not mirrored the true intent of God. Many fathers have chosen to abandon their responsibilities altogether by leaving while some have stayed and become great burdens. Where is the priest? What has he taught his children in the will and the ways of God? Who's praying on their behalf? Who is interceding for them? Who's standing in the gap for them? Fathers, what kind of generation are you producing?

3} SPOUSAL ABUSE & LOW SELF-ESTEEM

LEAH IS REJECTED BY JACOB

Laban, Leah's father said to Jacob in Genesis 29:27 says, *"Wait until the bridal week is over and you can have Rachel too – if you promise to work for me another seven years."* Jacob agreed. All he could think about was Rachel. He looked pass Leah, the woman he had just married and agreed to work another seven years for who he really wanted, Rachel.

Observation: He didn't want Leah! He didn't want her! Can you image that? Can you image being refused acknowledgement for who you are, not being received especially by someone you marry? Leah was now Jacob's wife and he wasn't accepting her as that; she wasn't who he loved, she wasn't who he longed for, she wasn't who he toiled seven years for, she wasn't who he spent time with in expectation of making her his very own. Jacob was betrothed to Rachel.

In the Jewish culture, betrothal was marriage and it took place in two stages. During the first stage, they were legally married but they didn't cohabit together. The wife remained with her family. That first period of betrothal was for seven years for Jacob and, coupled with the second, Rachel and Jacob's betrothal is known as the longest period of such in the scriptures. The betrothal was so serious in Jewish law it required a divorce to break it. Engaged parties were referred to as husband and wife in scripture (Deuteronomy 22:23, Matthew 1:19), which confirms the respectful view of engagement. It was completely different from courtship today. Jacob had real expectations.

Jacob loved Rachel before he asked Laban to marry her in Genesis 29:19. His love for her preceded the commitment to work for her hand in marriage. Because he was penniless and could not pay a dowry, he worked seven years for her. So, at the end of that time period Jacob is quite anxious for her and he had to ask for his bride. Genesis 29:21 reads, *"Then Jacob said to Laban, give me my wife, for my time is completed that I may go in to her."* In other words, I've wed your daughter Rachel. I've worked the seven years you've requested. Now it is time for me to have my wife!

A man was expected to spend at least a week with his new bride before marrying an additional wife. So for the sake of appearance, Jacob was asked to wait until the bridal week was up. That was the custom. It would have been an embarrassment to the family and humiliation for Leah had things not played out according to tradition. With the week being completed no one would be the wiser sensing discontent already on the home front. It was Laban's concern that no one know before the honeymoon was over the groom was already looking to marry again. But Laban created the situation by being dishonest. And in fact, Jacob was looking to wed again; probably in his mind, the only real marriage of the two.

Remember, Jacob and Leah had spent a night of intimacy.

Leah was the recipient of all his passion. Sunrise comes, and then like a tone of bricks, the weight of reality hits her. He didn't want Leah. The scriptures didn't say that he hated Leah or had disdain for her. But she was not who he wanted. Most of the time when people are rejected, instead of their position being, "Bye, see you later, or you don't know what you're missing, I'm a great catch," you start inspecting yourself wondering what's wrong with you that you're so undesirable. You start taking inventory to see what it is about yourself you can change so you will be desirable. Can I change my hair, my style of dress; am I too vocal, or too quiet. The burden of acceptance is now on you as opposed to the burden being on the person rejecting you. *That's what the enemy does. He makes you the offender when it is he who has committed the offense.*

Jacob and Leah are married but the union flies in the face of what marriages are intended to be. Leah has become a victim. She's not honored the way a wife should be honored. She's not loved the way a wife should be loved. She's being neglected. She is questioning her self-worth, and there may be some degree of shame. Because she's not alone with her husband in their own residence, but rather in a group family setting, *everybody knows* what's going on. She doesn't even have the comfort of hiding herself behind closed doors. Her embarrassment and humiliation are out front in the open for everyone to see. As a matter of fact, at the end of the week when Jacob finished his obligation, he marries Rachel and goes off to be with her. Leah is no more than an obligation to Jacob, but she has to accept some degree of responsibility for the conditions in which she finds herself. But let's not forget Laban and certainly not Jacob. Jacob is guilty of abusing Leah.

Spousal abuse can be physical. There is no evidence of such in our study here of Leah and Jacob. Physical abuse is most often easy to see. And when it occurs no one questions the victim's decision to end the relationship with the perpetrator. But what about when the abuse isn't obvious and the couple seems to have the perfect relationship? Often it is next to impossible to get help because of the perception of a healthy relationship. What happens when the perpetrator goes out of his or her way to make it seem as though everything is fine, thereby making the other party look as though they are making things up when trying to convey the difficulty that has been going on in the relationship. When I finally reached the point I knew I needed help, getting help was extremely difficult because I helped my spouse falsify our relationship. I was ashamed and didn't want anyone to know the truth of what really existed between my husband and me. And he counted on me not talking; he counted on me wanting everyone to think we were the perfect family, i.e. two children, a beautiful home, luxury car, dog, and the whole nine yards. There are a lot of unspoken, nonverbal mind games that go on in situations such as mine. Because of my skewed religious beliefs, and, because I didn't want my children to be the product of a broken family, I allowed the charade to go on for far too long. Everything looked perfect, but it wasn't. Help is harder to come by when no one believes what you're saying. At the point one begins to open up and expose the enemy, the abuse doesn't discontinue. It goes on and sometimes gets much worse because of the retribution, the retaliation for having said anything about the ongoing conditions. There is nothing worse than going to someone for help and they don't believe you. The enemy sits off somewhere laughing because all of it, what you're suffering, is a part of his game. The perpetrator comes off looking like the model husband, wife, father, mother, sister, whom ever they are. And those you talk to say things like, "You can't be talking about so-in-so. I've known them all my life and I've never known them to be thus and so." Well, there is any number of people in institutions now because people were not able to see individuals for who they really were thereby not giving the help that was so desperately needed. There are people in institutions now because someone couldn't take it any longer and decided this is it, the buck stops here. The enemy comes but to kill, steal, and destroy, (John 10:10). And as far as he's concerned, he has been successful because he has accomplished that end.

Emotional scars

Spousal abuse is not only manifested in physical abuse, it can be emotional as well, which oftentimes makes it harder to see. Emotional abuse includes verbal attacks, such as yelling, screaming, name-calling, but also the silent treatment. Using criticism, verbal threats, social isolation, neglect, intimidation or exploitation to dominate another person are other forms of emotional abuse. Being on the receiving end of emotional abuse can certainly lead to low self-esteem or no self-worth at all. Many of us have had the experience of feeling we haven't been "good enough" in a specific situation, particularly if we face rejection or criticism. But if what you feel about yourself is effected directly by what others feel about you, then you are suffering with low self-esteem. Of course, everyone cares to a certain extent about how others see you, but if it causes you to alter who you are, you are suffering with low self-esteem. Dr. Vijai P. Sharma, Ph.D. says in her article on 'The Negative Outcomes of Having Low Self-Esteem' to ask yourself the question: Do I respect myself? If you answered yes, then you have good self-esteem. If you answered no, then you don't.

Some intricacies of low self-esteem

Let's look at low self-esteem a little closer.
We have mistakenly thought people to sometimes be overly sensitive about the least little thing when in actuality their actions have been totally based on the fact they have low self-esteem. When you find yourself taking totally innocent comments by people and making them into something way more complex than the intent; turning the words into something hurtful at your expense, your self-esteem is very low. Not being able to sustain a relationship because you are so easily offended makes it quite difficult to have healthy fellowship with others leaving you abandoned and alone. You've become high maintenance and require those involved with you to exercise a very high level of energy just to even spend casual time together. People who are pessimistic about everything; looking and expecting whatever can go wrong will go wrong, spend their daily existence with a dark cloud of negativity always overshadowing them. This is where Leah was. Everything was wrong. She was married, separated and abandoned all in one week and somehow she felt responsible for everything, totally responsible for where life had taken her. Yes, she could have taken a stance and not be a party to all of the happenings, but it was not all on her, it wasn't all her doing.

4} VICTIMIZED - VICTIMIZER

As a victim of abuse, you have to be extremely careful you don't perpetuate the cycle of abuse. That cycle happens not only in families, but it can also happen when you're in a close relationship with anyone. Often times, an abuser comes from generations of abusers and they practice behavior that has become so familiar and comfortable to them. Familiar because when you are apart of something with such regularity, it comes to be subconsciously ingrained and even expected. So, with every action you come to know what the reaction will be because you've been there so many times before. But when you say someone becomes comfortable with abuse that means even though it is harmful, demeaning, and disruptive to ones life, you get use to it. You become placid or undisturbed and you settle yourself with the sate of mind that says, "This is just the way it is" or you think, it's really not that bad. You begin to know the patterns of abuse, and you begin to know the time element; you know how long before this incident runs its course, and the signs that indicate when this particular episode will all blow over.

You can pray and pray to God for so long, and when He sends His deliverance to you, you can become angry with Him because of the way He chooses to deliver you. As crazy as that sounded to me, I would never say nor entertain the idea that I was angry with God. I was too pious and self-righteous to ever say it. *But I was angry and I was being dishonest about it.* I was angry because I felt God turned what appeared to be my perfect world upside down. I say appeared perfect because there was nothing perfect about it but that was the perception I worked so hard to give. I was willing to keep on living in the state I was living in as long as no one knew the state I was living in. Perpetrators count on their victims remaining silent so I was in full compliance. That helps to protect them and aid them in their abuse; remain silent and no one will know. *There is only darkness in silence, but truth is in the light.* Since I wasn't going to be honest enough to tell God I was angry with Him, I likewise was not going to be overly receptive to Him or to whomever He sent to aid me in my deliverance. God can send someone who is angelic in their consistency to walk with you daily, pray for you continually, encourage you and be there for you. And in your frustration with God you can make them bare the brunt of the responsibility for what you are indirectly aiming at Him. What you've done is become the victimizer, the perpetrator, and the abuser. What you are doing is punishing them for being obedient to the voice of the Lord. How many times have we been guilty of killing the messenger? How many times have we rejected God when rejecting His message, His direction, and His guidance?

I Samuel 8:7 – *"And the LORD said unto Samuel, Hearken unto the voice of the people in all that they say unto thee: for they have not rejected thee, but they have rejected me, that I should not reign over them."*

I Samuel 10:19 – *"And ye have this day rejected your God, who*

Himself saved you out of all your adversities and your tribulations; and ye have said unto Him, Nay, but set a king over us. Now therefore present yourselves before the LORD by your tribes, and by your thousands." Samuel was grieved because in rejecting him as the voice of the Lord, Israel was rejecting God. And we reject those sent by God and cause them to feel the pain of the rejection intended for Him.

We must be careful how we treat those who are sent to be a blessing in our lives. God help us, because now there is someone that needs to be delivered from you; the messenger (the one sent by God for you) now needs deliverance. Make no mistake about it, God loves His messenger just as much as He loves you and He will not allow them to suffer at your hand just like He would not allow you to suffer at the hand of another. Own up to who you are, what you've become, what you are doing, and seek God so you may be freed from the bondage of sin. We can become so easily blinded by our own dilemmas, so consumed by our own challenges we fail to see what we may be doing to others. Look at yourself please, just as I was made to look at myself! Be strong enough to see who you've become. I've cautioned myself and now I caution those who continue to ignore the voice of the Lord and continue to refuse the direction He's giving for their lives. The Spirit of the Lord will not dwell with you always, certainly not under these conditions. I John 1:9 reads, *"If we confess our sins, He is faithful and just to forgive us our sins, and to cleanse us from all unrighteousness."* It is not His desire we die in the wilderness. We're assured through His word, *"I* (you) *shall not die, but live, and declare the works of the Lord. The Lord hath chastened me* (you) *sore: but He hath not given me over to death.'* Psalm 118:17-18, (emphasis added), "Hear Him and know He can bring you out of this place too." Prayer still works and there is nothing too hard for Him; *"For with God nothing shall be impossible"* Luke 1:37.

If you find yourself in a place the Spirit of the Lord is speaking to you, listen. Your difficulty right now is in trying to understand how you can be someone who's capable of inflicting such great pain. You see yourself as a good person, and I'm sure, undoubtedly you are. But now you've turned into what you've hated for so long; which is what makes the offense even greater. Let the Holy Spirit arrest your spirit so you can see; and I mean all of it. Yes, it's ugly, but you have to see. Yes, it's frightening, but you have to see it. Cry out at the reality of what you see, and then cry to God for the help you need.

Isaiah 55:6-7 reads, *"Seek ye the Lord while He may be found, call ye upon Him while He is near: let the wicked forsake his way, and the unrighteous man his thoughts: and let him return unto the Lord, and He will have mercy upon him; and to our God, for He will abundantly pardon."*

Your actions may not be deliberate but they are an offense nonetheless. Turn to God for help.

5} SIBLING RIVALRY

THE SISTER'S RELATIONSHIP WAS NO LONGER THE SAME

Genesis 29:28-30 reads, *"Jacob did so and fulfilled her week, and he gave him his daughter Rachel as his wife. Laban also gave his maid Bilhah to his daughter Rachel as her maid. So Jacob went in to Rachel also, and indeed he loved Rachel more than Leah, and he served with Laban for another seven years."* Jacob lived with Rachel right after he completed the mandatory seven days with Leah. And he began to work the second seven years so he might complete the agreement to have Rachel as his wife. Now, there is a third party in the Jacob/Leah relationship, that being Rachel and the love that once was pure and unadulterated is now *tainted* by competition.

Now, imagine the kind of tension that was going on between Rachel and Leah; both desiring the love and attention of the same man. Think of the amount of jealousy and envy that must have been present that may not have existed between them before all of this came about. Laban is the primary culprit in ruining the relationship between the two sisters, his two daughters. There was possibly some degree of strain between them growing up. The Bible describes Leah was weak-eyed and unattractive while Rachel was truly beautiful. Not only in our society is favor or advantages afforded to persons who are attractive, who have model-like shapes, who knows someone who knows someone, but this same sort of behavior is found in families too. How many times has it happened that a father prefers the athletic son over the brainy son? Or you may have the mother who favors the cheerleader daughter over the daughter in the science club. Jealousy between siblings grows out of the perception that one child is loved more than the other.

Jacob came from such a household, and could easily recognize the rivalry that existed between Rachel and Leah. And through personal experience, there were certainly some things he could have done to bring harmony between these sisters but he didn't. It is of major importance we look at the fact that Jacob was not only a major contributor in the abuse suffered by Rachel and Leah, but he too was a victim of abuse. Looking at his background, his family life, he grows up in a home where pitting one child against the other was the way his family functioned.

Isaac, Jacob's father, was the "Promised Seed" of God to Abraham and Sarah. The age of Isaac's parents was a major factor in Sarah trying to help God out in fulfilling His promise to her and Abraham. Sarah provided Haggai, her handmaiden as a surrogate mother in place of her old aging body. The product of the union between Haggai and Abraham was Ishmael, the source of great contention in the camp because of the jealousy spawn by his presence. After the arrival of Isaac, the two mothers continually promoted their sons for the express purpose of getting the attention and favor of the boy's father, Abraham. Isaac had two sons, Esau and Jacob. Isaac favors Esau because he was the outdoors, hunter type and fresh game was a delight to Isaac. On the other hand, Rebekah, the boy's mother favored Jacob, the indoor, stay around the house, readily available kind of person. God had spoken to Rebekah in a dream before her twin boys were born telling her the older child, Esau, who was delivered first, would serve the younger child, Jacob. But like her mother-in-law Sarah, Rebekah tried to help God out. She helped her son deceive his father into giving him the blessing of the "first born." And again because of impatience, not willing to wait on the timing and will of God, matters were made much worse than they ever had to be. This dysfunctional household, with each parent showing more attention to one child over the other was the basis for the continued perpetuation of misuse and wrong treatment that manifested itself through the life of the now adult child Jacob.

Verse 31 in Genesis 29 says, *"But because Jacob was slighting Leah, Jehovah let her have a child, while Rachel was barren."* <u>God saw Leah</u>. Just like God saw Leah, He sees us when we are in distress. And that is something He needs us to understand. He desires we know He's a loving and caring God and He gets no glory in our distress. Also, regardless of how isolated you may feel in your situation, God sees you. Your pain, your anxiety, and your hurts are all seen and felt by God. And He moves on your behalf.

Psalm 18:6 says, *"In my distress I called upon the Lord, and cried unto my God: He heard my voice out of His temple, and my cry came before Him, even into His ears."* Our cries of distress may be simply, "Oh Lord," or in a moan, a heavy sigh or in our tears. And while it is we may not have consciously called out to God, our spirit calls out to Him. God wants us to look to Him. Psalm 27:5 reads, *"For in the time of trouble He shall hide me in His pavilion: in the secret of His tabernacle shall He hide me; He shall set me up upon a rock."* Distress can give you such a feeling of helplessness, such a feeling of *forged* settlement or resolve, meaning, this is the way it is and I see no way out. But God sees and He knows. I remember that feeling of helplessness being in a horrible marriage for so long. I remember looking at my age, thinking about how long people were living and guessing how long I would probably have to live being so very unhappy. It was God who said, "Enough is enough!" I was prepared to remain in that state but God said, "No, you're my child and I will not allow you to live in this condition any longer. I've gone to your spouse many times, and not only is he rejecting you, he is rejecting me."

There is no question Leah was a victim of circumstances. The conditions of abuse were very real. But even in all of what she was suffering, *God was trying to get her attention to let her know,* **"I am with you."**

We see glimpses of God getting through to her and her acknowledgement of that in the naming of her children. God blessed her with her first son, *Reuben* whose name meant, *"God has noticed my trouble."* She named her next son *Simeon* meaning, *"Jehovah heard."* He knew that I (Leah) was unloved and gave me another son. But yet Leah is struggling and is not able to get the breakthrough she needs to receive her restoration from God. So, in the naming of her third son, *Levi* meaning, *"Attachment."* Leah felt, surely now my husband will feel affection for me, since I have given him three sons. She again switches her attention away from God to that of Jacob. Then with the next child, Leah turns back to God for she names him *Judah, "Praise...for now I will praise Jehovah."*

Leah was looking for emotional love, while God was trying to give her divine love. *She was not responding to the person who loved her above all others.* Emotional love can change as conditions change but God's divine love never changes. He's the same yesterday, today, and forever more. He says, I will love you with an everlasting love (Jeremiah 31:3). And there is no shadow of turning with God. He is a constant, consistent God. Even when we're not being loving, He yet loves us. With the naming of Judah, Leah was finally saying, this time I will praise the Lord. *She turned from yearning the emotional love of Jacob to receiving the divine love of God.*

6} THE ABUSE OF OMISSION

At this juncture I must discuss with you another aspect of abuse we probably would have a hard time seeing or even agreeing with.

In the beginning of our discussion, in our definitions of abuse, one of the meanings given is, "…to treat in a harmful way." Now, I want you to look at the reality of the fact that when we don't introduce our children to Christ in a meaningful way, when we're not active in our guidance into the knowledge and truth of who God is, we are treating them in a harmful way. You may question how such a statement could be made. You may naturally say there is no physical or mental abuse. You are right it's not physical or mental abuse but revealed to me that this is spiritual abuse. What have we told our children about God? Do they see Him as anything other than someone you give vague reference to? Our society has raised a generation of youths that have no serious interaction with our Savior and Lord, which primarily has been the case because *they don't know Him*. The first introduction to God comes in the home by the parents through the consciousness that He is a rewarder of them that diligently seek Him. We teach them He is the creator of the universe and mankind. But how many of us teach them Jesus Christ is the Son of God and He willingly gave His life to save us from sin? How many of us tell them

God the Father desires we have a relationship with Him and we need to communicate with Him daily? How many of us tell our children hell is a real place and for those of us who make the decision that we don't need God or His Son, we'll find eternity to be a place of never ending torment? A parent was recently quoted in an article in the Washington Post as having said to his wife, "I don't want you to expose my daughters to some fictitious God." He didn't believe in God and didn't want to expose his children to God either. We harm them by not giving them the opportunity to spend eternity with God!

Some of you are shaking your heads right now, calling this extremely harsh and dark but our children are exposed to all manner of evil by Satan and the wickedness of the world through every medium imaginable. Yet, when it comes to things pertaining to God, our faith and incorporating it as a priority in the lives of our children we're often accused of brainwashing and abuse. If you notice, the laws are being developed to work against our scriptural instructions and insight from the Spirit. I've heard so many parents say, "I'll let my children decide for themselves when they're old enough." You and I both know whatever you don't expose them to or demonstrate on a daily basis does not exist in the minds of our kids. Society, especially social media and television has found a way to effectively persuade our children to grab on to whatever the latest 'thing' is in hopes of being in the know and accepted among those who for the most part do not care anything about them. Courage is urgently needed among parents, our kids suffer for lack of it!

In almost identical ways, we have failed our children just as the children of Israel failed theirs. They didn't teach their sons and daughters about God and consequently they continually sinned because they lacked the knowledge of who God was. Moses tells the children of Israel in Deuteronomy 11:19-21 (NLT), "Teach them to your children. Talk about them when you are at home and when you are on the road, when you are going to bed and when you are getting up. Write them on the doorposts of your house and on your gates, so that as long as the sky remains above the earth, you and your children may flourish in the land the LORD swore to give your ancestors." What He's telling them and now us is we have to teach our children who God is. Instruct them in your faith. Tell them what it is God has done for you, i.e., He brought you out of bondage in Egypt. He opened the Red Sea and delivered you to the other side. He fed you with manna from heaven. He guided you with a cloud by day and fire by night. Discuss the magnificence of who God is so they will come to know Him and love Him too. Testify to your children so they will know Him to be more than the God of the Bible. He's healed you from very traumatic diseases, the homes you own are yours because God made it so when creditors would not. Your tenure on your job is inexplicable when cut backs have diminished the workforce around you. The fact that you've been able to maintain your sanity is because God Himself cradled you and nursed you through the devastating period of your life. Your education has not opened the floodgates of opportunity for you, but the favor of God has moved you into areas your qualifications would not have taken you. Tell your children, they must know. God has been great in your life and if you don't tell them they won't know. Israel didn't do as they were instructed and as a result of them not taking an active role in rehearsing the things God had done, their children did not know Him, and in the Judges period they continually sinned. They became entangled in the culture of the land, started worshipping false gods, and forsook the God of their people. Their behavior denigrated into a cycle of disobedience. They would sin, God would send an oppressor to punish them, they'd repent, and then God would deliver them; once they felt God's mercy, sin began all over again. This cycle went on over a long period of time but yet resulted in the children (the new generation) entering the Promised Land, gaining needed experience through hardship. Israel *finally* came to know who God was.

Are we teaching our children who God is? As we ride in the car, as we sit at mealtime, when we're walking in the mall do we talk about God? Do we pray a meaningful prayer of covering over them, with their participation, as they leave our presence? In other words, when we go about our daily routines, do we reinforce our faith? This is such a serious matter and our children are our single most important investment into the body of Christ; an investment we make for years to come. Training up a soldier to do battle for our King! Of course, our active participation in the Kingdom is ongoing, but now is the time to train the militiamen to fight against the advancement of the enemy. We train them now that they may lock arms with us in our work to reveal the defeated foe and snatch back those who have fallen prey to his unrelenting army. Going to church is not enough. Singing in the choir is not enough. Participation in Christmas and Easter programs is not enough. These activities serve to reinforce that which we are teaching our children, not the sole source of what they hear about Christ.

Our children need to know we were created to serve God. Like Israel, we are that city that sits upon a hill that cannot be hid, (Matthew 5:14). Meaning, the might of God shines through who we are. Before He created us, He knew us and designed us with a purpose. But how will our children reach their destiny if we don't acquaint them with the One who designed who they would be before they came to be?

Of course, when our children get older, they make choices and decisions for themselves, but we have to help them make *informed* decisions. We have to help them acknowledge there is a heaven for those who accept Christ as Lord and King and to know there is a hell for those who choose not to. We have to help them know and acknowledge that God is the lover of their souls and no good thing will He withhold from them if they walk upright before Him. What Satan offers is fake, counterfeit, temporary, and will fade away. We have to help them come to the knowledge of the truth that Jesus Christ is the way.

7} GODLY RESTORATION

GOD CAN RESTORE US TO WHO HE CREATED US TO BE

God is with us in our struggles. Regardless as to what is being said to us or about us, regardless as to how we are being made to feel, regardless as to how we are not appreciated for our worth, or how the strain of survival has changed us; God can restore us to who He created us to be. Abuse can make us someone who we are not. Abuse can make us hard, distant, removed, callous, empty, indifferent, mean, evil, appeasing, too accommodating and/or anything that expresses itself in an excessive way.

In spite of all Jehovah God was doing for Leah, her self worth, in her mind, was tied into being validated by her husband through his love. Leah was performing her wifely duties and had reasonable hopes and expectations. I recognize the bond and love that is to take place in a husband/wife relationship, but no one defines who you are but God. There's that part of you that houses your make-up; your spirit, your innermost being. And in relationships, no one is to have access to that person *but God*. We are expecting from people that which can only come from God. The act of validating a person is authority no one should have over another, no one but God. As a member of a relational unit, we have expectations, and we want to be

33

Fight to Get YOU Back

loved and appreciated, but God and only God validates who you are. For many of you there is a void, which you expect to be filled in other places, but that filling can only come from God. Even when the relationship appears to be right, what belongs to God belongs to God. And I caution you not to give it away. We are allowing others to have an authority over us that's intended for God and God alone. We have raised up lords in our lives and they threaten the place God has reserved and ordained for Himself. Exodus 20:3 and 5 read, *"Thou shalt have no other gods before me. Thou shalt not bow down thyself to them, nor serve them; for I the Lord thy God am a jealous God."* I feel strongly about this. Please listen to someone who was, at one point in my life, totally consumed by another person. I gave that person the reigns of my life and when I tried to get them back I couldn't. God had to rescue me. And it's not always people. We also try to feel voids in our lives with addictions, i.e., food, pornography, gambling, following false doctrines, etc.

Rachel finally has children and the naming of her children too is reflective of the struggle, contention and rivalry between herself and her sister, Leah. A very important issue to note in Rachel's cry for children is made by Jacob after she has been crying and begging. *"Give me children or I'll die."* Jacob's accurate response is, *"Am I God?"* In other words, you are looking for me to give you something only God can give. As was the case with Rachel, we look to people for that which only comes from God. We suffer with displaced devotion. An excellent paraphrase of Exodus 20:3 and 5 says, *"Don't do it. Look only to Me, the Lord your God."* Rachel and Leah lost the essence of who they were in their quest to find total fulfillment in their relationship with another, namely their husband.

Who are you? You may be a mother, a sister, a wife, a daughter, a co-worker, a father, a husband, a son, a friend, an employee or a leader. But that's not who you are. That's the role you play. Who are you? What I mean is, who did God create when He created you; who did He create you to be? When God looks at you He doesn't see the 'You' others see, but He sees who He created you to be. Jeremiah 1:15 reads, *"Before I formed thee in the belly I knew thee; and before thou camest forth out of the womb I sanctified thee, and I ordained thee a prophet unto the nations."* You have a purpose and that purpose is not to be abused by your family or anyone else. He handcrafted us with our God-given abilities to do something unique for Him. You may share the same parents as someone else, you may share the same street address as someone else, and you may even have the same facial appearance as someone else. But *there is no one else like you in the entire world.*

You may be a far cry from the 'You' God created you to be, but there is nothing too hard for God. All He needs is for you not to give up on yourself. Come boldly to Him that you can find the help you need. If you suffer with physical abuse, He can help you. If you have to hear the ranting and ravings daily that you are a piece of trash, good for nothing, He can help you. If you've been made to feel you're the dumbest person ever to walk the face of this earth, He can help you. If you are physically being violated daily by family member or quasi-family members, He can help you. If you are neglected to the point there is no real love shown and your emotions cry out just for someone to care, He can help you and make sure you become the person He created you to be.

Ephesians 1:4 says, *"According as He hath chosen us in Him before the foundation of the world, that we should be holy and without blame before Him in love."* So, who am I? I'm the chosen, I'm without blame and I'm loved. Romans 8:16 says, *"The Spirit itself beareth witness with our spirit, that we are the children of God."* Who am I? I am a child of God. Revelations 1:6, *"And hath made us kings and priests unto God and His Father; to Him be glory and dominion for ever and ever."* Who am I? I am a king, a queen and a priest unto God. Galatians 3:29, *"And if ye be Christ's, then are you Abraham's seed, and heirs according to the promise."* Who am I? I am Abraham's seed, and an heir. I Peter 2:9, *"But ye are a chosen generation, a royal priesthood, an holy nation, a peculiar people: that ye should shew forth the praises of Him who hath called you out of darkness into His marvelous light."* God's Word tells us who we are and who He made us to be.

God wants to deliver us from whatever state we find ourselves in. If you were sick and the local clinic was offering free health care, and all you had to do was go to the clinic to receive help, wouldn't you go? Office hours are open! Allow God to give you a trustworthy person with whom you can talk to without threat of repercussions or betrayal; someone who will manifest Him. If by chance there is need for more professional clinical help, I highly recommend the American Association of Christian Counselors (AACC) or you may be able to access what's available to you by going online and search for them, key word being "Christian counselor." However, I admonish you to stay prayerful as you seek help. Be assured, God, the great physician and healer is able to cure all manner of disease, sickness, hurts, and pains. You need only to come to Him and open up your heart completely; talk to Him.

Yes, God knows all, but He wants us to talk to Him so the healing process can begin. It is very important to remember, whichever course of action you elect to take, allow God to be at the center of it. He made you and He has the design. And only He can restore you to the masterful artwork He created you to be.

8} FIGHT TO GET YOU BACK

WHY THE FIGHT?

One of the hardest realities I ever faced was understanding how much I collaborated with Satan in my own demise. I had to take responsibility for opening the door that allowed the abuse I suffered; it was my own doing. Oh, I spent time playing the blame game; but when I finally looked in my heart of hearts, I had to be honest and accept the fact it was me. Being too trusting of others, wearing my innocence like a badge of honor alerted the enemy to my culpability. There was no honor in not being mature, in an innocence that wasn't a God type of innocence. I had a pure heart always looking to see the best, in people…in circumstances. I haven't stopped looking but now I look with a maturity of heart in being aware of the realities of life and understanding the relentlessness of the enemy.

2 Corinthians 10:4, *"For the weapons of our warfare are not carnal, but mighty through God to the pulling down of strong holds."* I was no good to God, myself or anyone else not recognizing the futility of my fairytale existence. I couldn't fight; I was blind to the fight. There's a war going on and Satan is rendering so many of us as invalids through voluntary ignorance. The longer he can keep you in that place you're not a threat to him or the forces of hell. The

enemy doesn't care how he renders you useless, he just wants you futile, worthless and ineffective.

2 Timothy 3:5 (NLT) reads, *"They will act religious, but they will reject the power that could make them godly. Stay away from people like that!"* When we lose ourselves it's because we've rejected the power that makes us strong; the power that keeps us connected to the almighty King. Being connected to church does not make you connected to God; attendance, going through the formalities, tithe paying and the like has nothing to do with being in fellowship with Him and has given so many a false sense of security. Church and God are not synonymous.

God constantly speaks to us through His Word. Psalm 73:28 (NLT), *"But as for me, it is good to be near God. I have made the Sovereign LORD my refuge; I will tell of all your deeds."* Happiness, comfort, security, love, success and the like are found in JESUS alone! Put ALL your trust in Him!

Psalm 118:17, *"I shall not die, but live, and declare the works of the LORD."* Your determination has to be, 'Find God and live.' The enemy's sole purpose is to make sure you never find Him so you won't live or live so far beneath the life Jesus died for you to have. God's promise is, if you stretch your hand towards Me, I'll reach out and grab it. Fight for your life!

Who are you fighting?

Your greatest fight is with yourself. I know that ignited something in you, you didn't want to hear or feel but it's true. No, you weren't the catalyst for all the negative things that have led to this place of defeat, but you embraced them.

You've been conducive to the things that have kept you off kilter and off balance. You weren't saying the words and you weren't performing the actions but you accepted them and gave life to them. You nourished those seeds of doubt and ineffectiveness, disillusionment and ineptitude, not being good enough and disqualification; you let them lie there with no effort to rid yourself, not brushing them away and finally, letting them take root. *They were camouflaged; you couldn't see them for what they were, your spiritual eyes were dim because of your distance from God.* Consequently, they're entrenched, and now everything you do is the effected by your inaction; your vantage point is clouded with the untruths spoken by the enemy's agents. They kept talking because you kept listening. They kept performing because you kept looking. Now, you close your ears and still hear them, shut your eyes and still see them. You have to regain control of you! You can no longer be a willing audience. If Eve had stayed close to God she would have had the strength to walk away when Satan came to entice her.

There is something about us, in our human nature, in our DNA that makes us think things are different when it comes to us. We often feel, because we're special, the course that has already been laid by God's direction, will be altered to accommodate us. An exception is in order because "It's me"

Lord. That kind of thinking has you repeating the same mistakes over and over again because you don't feel as though you have to toe the line and do it the way God says. Choosing to be stuck on stupid will not invoke sympathy or mercy and will find you running out of God's great grace. Continuing to walk in your own way is equivalent to beating your head against a brick wall; it will be very painful, and still it won't render the results you're looking for. Get to God! II Chronicles 7:14 says, *"If my people, which are called by my name, shall humble themselves, and pray, and seek my face, and turn from their wicked ways; then will I hear from heaven, and will forgive their sin, and will heal their land."*

Fight to get yourself out of the grips of the enemy. Fight to understand your worth in God. Fight to accept God's love for you and come back to the knowledge He sent His Son to die for you. No greater love, John 15:13, *"Greater love hath no man than this, that a man lay down his life for his friends."*

HOW DO YOU FIGHT?

To get you back, the fight is both in the physical and spiritual realms; and *you, through God, are the one initiating the fight*. You are no longer running out of fear from the enemy, you are now on the offensive, determined to get you back; the you God created you to be.

Here are the five (5) FIGHT Principles given to me by GOD. (I keep them before me daily):

1) *You have to fully cooperate with God*

41

It's a misnomer to think God does all the work to free you from the grip of the enemy and you just stand idly by waiting for Him to finish so you can just walk right into the blessing He provided. That way of thinking is a trick of the enemy as well. I've heard so many say, "You know it is God when there's no struggle and everything falls right into place." There are a few occasions when that's true, but many more when it's not. We suffer from the false belief that if there's a fight, it's not God. But not only is He fighting on our behalf, God leads the charge and the Heavenly Host is His army. Our cooperation with Him is what ensures we triumph, we win. Lack of cooperation ensures our defeat.

2) *You are responsible for walking out the manifested work of God*

Again, God does the work, does the healing, delivers you and gives you victory. But here's the clincher and this is where you come in. You are responsible for walking out what God has made manifest in your life. Your walk with Him, your faithfulness, and your complete compliance to His work is what allows you to actually see what you're looking for to, *come to pass.* "The work is already done!" How many times have you heard that? So then, you ask yourself, "Why am I not seeing it?" You don't see it because you're not positioned to see it; often we get lackadaisical in our walk. We're inconsistent; we don't follow through. We're on point one minute and can't be found the next; *we want to shout the victory and not walk the victory.* We're impatient and want everything right now. God doesn't work like that and coming to that realization unlocks our understanding for the need to *stay focused until it's finished. Inconsistency makes you weak and being weak makes you unfit for battle.*

Your spiritual muscles have to be built before the real battle takes place. Your confidence in the God of deliverance takes place from the small victories you experience along the way. *Do what God says <u>daily</u>.* Follow Him in a very real and practical way. Fight to stay on track. Victories come from fighting and fighting comes from not settling anymore; the warrior has to be awakened in you.

Deuteronomy 1:8 reads, *"Behold, I have set the land before you: go in and possess the land which the LORD sware unto your fathers, Abraham, Isaac, and Jacob, to give unto them and to their seed after them."* Here's the thing, there were people already occupying the land and they weren't going to let Israel come in and inhabit it. But God said He'd given it to them. He had, they were assured victory when they fought to possess it. That was Israel's part; the fight brought the manifestation of the victory God had promised. Fight! Don't wander aimlessly in the desert because of fear, indecision, disobedience and stubbornness. Guarantee the victory in worshipping God and God alone.

3) *You have to silence the voice of the enemy by no longer listening to him*

Silencing the enemy may mean separation; you may have to distance yourself from those whose voices are not in alignment with God. A day or two out of contact is not silencing him; it may require months or even years. No longer keep company with those who aren't interested in seeing you made complete and whole. Let God select company keepers for you; those He can trust to be with you.

Replace the voice of the enemy with the voice of God. You'll recognize it because it completely aligns itself with what He's already said in scripture. *"…whatsoever things are true, whatsoever things are honest, whatsoever things are just, whatsoever things are pure, whatsoever things are lovely, whatsoever things are of good report; if there be any virtue, and if there be any praise, think on these things."* [Philippians 4:8]

"Thy word have I hid in mine heart, that I might not sin against thee" [Psalm 119:11]

4) *Stay before the Lord*

Consciously seeking God's face in His Word is how you fight; true repentance, fellowship, fasting and praying. Joel 2:12 & 13 (NIV), *"Yet even now, declares the LORD, "Return to Me with all your heart, and with fasting, weeping and mourning; and rend your heart and not your garments. Now return to the LORD your God, for He is gracious and compassionate, Slow to anger, abounding in lovingkindness and relenting of evil."*

Psalm 50:15 (NLT), *"Call upon me in the day of trouble; I will deliver you, and you will honor me."*

Hebrews 11:6, *"…he is a rewarder of them that diligently seek him…"* You may be in a place that looks so bleak and impossible, but *nothing is too hard for God*. Fight!

9} WORKS – PRODUCED BY THE FLESH

Every negative attribute we see in Laban and Jacob's family is the result of a lack of communion and fellowship with God, which conversely opens the door to cooperation and collaboration with Satan. No good thing ever comes from co-mingling our lives with the great deceiver, the malicious liar, and the diabolical pursuer of mankind. He entangles man with the attributes distinctive of himself in order to keep us from attaining and maintaining the characteristics of God. Marriage and family are ordained by God and He desires it be so as stated in His Word, Genesis 2:24 says, *"Therefore shall a man leave his father and his mother, and shall cleave unto his wife: and they shall be one flesh."* God follows by saying in Genesis 9:7, *"And you, be fruitful and multiply, bring forth abundantly on the earth and multiply in it."* It was in the plan of God from the beginning, i.e., get married, have a family. As in all things, the enemy wants to wreak havoc and bring destruction to the perfect will of God or simply anything associated with God.

God *ordained* family. It is here, in this unit, you have the nurturing of belief in Him. It's here in this unit you experience the purity and safety of the sharing of hearts, and the exploration of minds. Here is where you begin to understand the beauty and the order of life, the flow of relationships, and the sovereignty of God. Family is where

God planned for you to receive His divine love in an earthly existence. His love through the father, His love through the mother, sister, brother; God's love flourishing through the family, is a microcosm of the world as He intended. Relate, share, interact, accept, exchange, teach, mend, heal; all these things right here in the family. With God putting so much into it, Satan targets marriage and family to drain every inch of goodness out of it BEFORE we can benefit from it.

The foundational structure of the church and our society is the family. A sick disjointed family produces a church and society in much need of healing. Any strategic plan to dismantle or debilitate these institutions lies in the opposition's strength to divide and conquer. You've heard it many times, the family that prays together, stays together. So, the family that is not centered by God is subject to mass destruction. The family where there is no peace, where there is no love, and where there is no security lacks the godly cohesiveness that makes the structure strong.

Let's look at the negative attributes, or the works of the flesh the enemy used to poison the lives of Laban, Jacob, Rachel, and Leah. In this one family we see so much misfortune reflected in how they all relate to one another. Galatians 5:19 says, *"Now the works of the flesh are manifest, which are these; adultery, fornication, uncleanness, lasciviousness, idolatry, witchcraft, hatred, variance, emulations, wrath, strife, seditions, heresies, envyings, murders, drunkenness, revelings, and such like: of the which I tell you before, as I have also told you in time past, that they which do such things shall not inherit the kingdom of God."* Notice the phrase: "…and such like." Paul is saying, this list is not exhaustive. Any behavior that is not a result of your connection to God is behavior spawned by the enemy; as we'll see very clearly in this concise list of fruit produced by the flesh.

Works of the Flesh:

1. J<small>EALOUSY</small> – **resentful, envious, inclined to rivalry.**

   God's Word says:
   "Wherefore laying aside all malice, and all guile, and hypocrisies, and envies, and all evil speakings, as newborn babes, desire the sincere milk of the word, that ye may grow thereby."
   I Peter 2: 1 & 2

   "Let us not be desirous of vain glory, provoking one another, envying one another." Galatians 5:26

2. E<small>NVY</small> – **desire for another's advantages, discontent and dissatisfaction of one's attributes, possessions or position.**

   God's Word says:
   "For where envying and strife is, there is confusion and every evil work." James 3:16

   "For ye are yet carnal: for whereas there is among you envying, and strife, and divisions, are ye not carnal, and walk as men."
   I Corinthians 3:3

3. I<small>NSECURITY</small> – **subject to fears and doubts; uncertainty, suspicion.**

God's Word says:

"There is no fear in love: but perfect love casteth out fear: because fear hath torment. He that feareth is not made perfect in love."
I John 4:18

"In God have I put my trust: I will not be afraid what man can do unto me." Psalm 56:11

4. <u>LONELINESS</u> – **a depressing feeling of being alone**

God's Word says:

"I will not leave you comfortless: I will come to you." John 14:18

"Fear thou not; for I am with thee: be not dismayed; for I am thy God: I will strengthen thee; yea, I will help thee; yea, I will uphold thee with the right hand of my righteousness." Isaiah 41:10

5. <u>LOVELESS</u> –**lacking a profoundly tender, passionate affection for another person, without an intense personal attachment.**

God's Word says:

"As the Father hath loved me, so have I loved you: continue ye in my love. If ye keep my commandments, ye shall abide in my love; even as I have kept my Father's commandments, and abide in his love. These things have I spoken unto you, that my joy might remain in you, and that your joy might be full. This is my commandment that ye love one another, as I have loved you. Greater love hath no man than this, that a man lay down his life for his

friends…These things I command you, that ye love one another." John 15:9-13, 17

6. <u>DISHONESTY</u> – **untrustworthy, disposed to lying and cheating; lack of trust, lack of confidence.**

   God's Word says:
   "In thee, O Lord, do I put my trust: let me never be put to confusion." Psalm 71:1

   "God forbid: yea, let God be true, but every man a liar; as it is written, that thou mightest be justified in thy sayings, and mightest overcome when thou art judged." Romans 3:4

7. <u>GREED</u> – **excessive and without godly boundaries or an extreme carnal desire for wealth.**

   God's Word says:
   "Yea, they are greedy dogs which can never have enough, and they are shepherds that cannot understand: they all look to their own way, every one for his gain, for his quarter." Isaiah 56:11

   "He that is greedy of gain troubleth his own house; but he that hateth gifts shall live." Proverbs 15:27

8. <u>MANIPULATION</u> – **to manage or influence skillfully and often unfairly.**

   God's Word says:
   "Let no man deceive you with vain words: for because of these things cometh the wrath of God upon the children of

disobedience." Ephesians 5:6

"Little children, let no man deceive you: he that doeth righteousness is righteous, even as he is righteous. He that committeth sin is of the devil." I John 3: 7 & 8a

9. <u>DISAPPOINTMENT</u> – **to fail to fulfill expectations or wishes; failure to meet that which is anticipated.**

God's Word says:
"For all the promises of God in him are yea, and in him Amen, unto the glory of God by us." II Corinthians 1:20

"Trust ye in the Lord forever: for in the Lord Jehovah is everlasting strength." Isaiah 26:4

10. <u>DECEPTION</u> – **to mislead by false appearance or statement; to trick.**

God's Word says:
"Ye are of your father the devil, and the lusts of your father ye will do. He was a murderer from the beginning, and abode not in the truth, because there is no truth in him. When he speaketh a lie, he speaketh of his own: for he is a liar, and the father of it." John 8:44

"Lie not one to another, seeing that ye have put off the old man with his deed; and have put on the new man which is renewed in knowledge after the image of Him that created him." Colossians 3:9 & 10

11. <u>COMPETITION</u> – **to vie with another for or as if for a prize, contest   between rivals.**

    God's Word says:
    "If it be possible, as much as lieth in you, live peaceably with all men." Romans 12:18

    "Depart from evil, and do good, seek peace, and pursue it." Psalm 34:14

12. <u>FAVORITISM</u> – **partiality; prefer; special privilege or right granted.**

    God's Word says:
    "Favor is deceitful, and beauty is vain: but a woman that feareth the Lord, she shall be praised." Proverbs 31:30

    "A good man obtaineth favor of the Lord: but a man of wicked devices will He condemn." Proverbs 12:2

13. <u>BETRAYAL</u> – **to deliver to an enemy by treachery; to fail or desert in time of need.**

    God's Word says:
    "Now I beseech you, brethren, mark them which cause divisions and offences contrary to the doctrine which ye have learned; and avoid them. For they that are such serve not our Lord Jesus Christ, but their own belly; and by good words and fair speeches deceive the hearts of the simple." Romans 16:17 & 18

    "That we henceforth be no more children, tossed to and fro,

and carried about with every wind of doctrine, by the sleight of men, and cunning craftiness, whereby they lie in wait to deceive; but speaking the truth in love, my grow up into Him in all things, which is the head, even Christ."
Ephesians 4:14 & 15

Any conditions or situations that make you feel or operate under these influences are not of God. Anyone that walks in the flesh will not inherit the Kingdom of God. This is true for those who have not accepted Christ as their Lord and Savior and for those who say they have but are still greatly swayed by the enemy. The fruit that appears in our lives is an outward manifestation of inward growth or lack thereof. Whether the seed produces negative fruit or positive fruit, the truth of the matter is it started as a seed and had to have been fed soil and water to grow (whether good or bad). It didn't just pop up, there was a gestation process that took place, a time of conception and development. So, when it's there, it is there because we've allowed it to be. It is important to know no one is immune from the attacks of the enemy, even when he tries to sow seeds that will later produce hatred, envy, malice and "such like." But God will show you, if you let Him, when something is taking root in your heart. He will give us a 'heads up.' Look out, something there is not right. And if we ignore what the Spirit of God is saying to us, we can find ourselves in a quagmire that will mandate some intense fasting and prayer to pull us out. We have to work *in cooperation with God* for ultimately it is He that does the work. *"For it is God which worketh in you both to will and to do of his good pleasure."* Philippians 2:13.

10} FRUIT – PRODUCED BY THE SPIRIT

Conversely, God says, in Galatians 5:22, *"But the fruit of the Spirit is love, joy, peace, longsuffering, gentleness, goodness, faith, meekness, temperance: against such there is no law."* Again, "such" means this list is not exhaustive but includes the staples of righteous producing behavior. The word or mention of 'righteous' is often viewed with disdain and equally imposed by Pharisee-types who live in hopes that most will miss God rather than see themselves through the 'eyes of God.' Righteous at a base level means – in 'right-standing' with God; a work accomplished through the blood of our Lord Jesus Christ.

Do you notice the scripture says the "fruit" singularly of the Spirit? What the word is saying is there is one fruit and the essence of that fruit, or the core of that fruit is "love"; everything else is an offshoot from it. Just like a tree, love is considered the base or the trunk of the tree while joy, peace, longsuffering, gentleness, goodness, faith, meekness, and temperance are considered the branches of that tree. Love produces all the rest. When we walk in the spirit, the production of our fruit is good, not rotten, or spoiled, but good! When we have love, all of the other graces, if you will, are there for the developing. Any behavior that is a result of your connection to God is a discipline produced by adhering to the Word and yielding to the Holy Spirit. Let's take a more in-depth look at the fruit and what God says:

1. <u>LOVE</u> – **an unselfish concern that freely accepts another in loyalty and seeks his good.**

    God's Word says:
    "Love is patient and kind; love is not jealous or boastful; it is not arrogant or rude. Love does not insist on its own way; it is not irritable or resentful; it does not rejoice at wrong, but rejoices in the right. Love bears all things, believes all things, hopes all things, endures all things. Love never ends…" I Corinthians 13:4-7

    "For God so loved the world that He gave His only Son, that whoever believes in Him should not perish but have eternal life." John 3:16

2. <u>JOY</u> – **a constant state of happiness, a feeling of well-being.**

    God's Word says:
    "…for the joy of the Lord is your strength." Nehemiah 9:10

    "Yea, our heart is glad in Him, because we trust in His holy name. Let thy steadfast love, O Lord, be upon us, even as we hope in thee." Psalm 33:21 & 22

3. <u>PEACE</u> – **freedom from disquieting or oppressive thoughts or emotions; inner tranquility of heart, mind, and soul.**

God's Word says:
"May the LORD give strength to His people! May the Lord bless His people with peace." Psalm 29:11

"May the God of hope fill you with all joy and peace in believing, so that by the power of the Holy Spirit you may abound in hope." Romans 15:13

4. <u>LONGSUFFERING</u> **(patience) – long and patient endurance.**

God's Word says:
"May you be strengthened with all power, according to His glorious might, for all endurance and patience with joy." Colossians 1:11

"With all lowliness and meekness, with patience, forbearing one another in love." Ephesians 4:2

5. <u>GENTLENESS</u> **(kindness) – kind, not harsh, stern or violent; restrained; showing love and respect for others.**

God's Word says:
"And be kind to one another, tenderhearted, forgiving one another, as God in Christ forgave you." Ephesians 4:32

"By purity, knowledge, forbearance, kindness, the Holy Spirit, genuine love, truthful speech, and the power of God; with the weapons of righteousness for the right hand and

for the left."
II Corinthians 6:6 & 7

6. <u>GOODNESS</u> – **praiseworthy character, excellence, virtue.**

God's Word says:
"Wherefore also we pray always for you, that our God would count you worthy of this calling, and fulfill all the good pleasure of His goodness, and the work of faith with power." II Thessalonians 1:11

"For the fruit of the Spirit is in all goodness and righteousness and truth." Ephesians 5:9

7. <u>FAITH</u> **(faithful) – steadfast in affection or allegiance.**

God's Word says:
"O LORD, I will honor and praise your name, for you are my God. You do such wonderful things! You planned them long ago, and now you have accomplished them." Isaiah 25:1

"That according to the riches of His glory He may grant you to be strengthened with might though His Spirit in the inner man, and that Christ may dwell in your hearts through faith; that you, being rooted and grounded in love. May be able to comprehend with all saints what is the breadth, and length, and depth, and height; and to know the love of Christ, which passeth knowledge, that ye might be filled with all the fullness of God." Ephesians 3:16-19

8. <u>MEEKNESS</u> – enduring injury with patience and without resentment complimented by spiritual guidance and instruction.

God's Word says:
"Blessed are the meek: for they shall inherit the earth." Matthew 5:5

"Brethren, if a man be overtaken in a fault, ye which are spiritual, restore such an one in the spirit of meekness; considering thyself, lest thou also be tempted." Galatians 6:1

9. <u>TEMPERANCE</u> (self-control) – moderation in action, thought, or feeling; restraint, control over ones actions.

God's Word says:
"And beside this, giving all diligence, add to your faith virtue; and to virtue knowledge; and to knowledge temperance; and to temperance patience; and to patience godliness." II Peter 1:5-7

"As we have therefore opportunity, let us do good unto all men, especially unto them who are of the household of faith." Galatians 6:10

The fruit of the Spirit are the characteristics of Christ. God seeks daily to have us look more and more like His son, Jesus Christ; may we seek the Lord daily in our desire to be molded in His likeness.

11} HE HAS THE FINAL SAY

Jeremiah 29:11 (NIV) reads, *"For I know the plans I have for you* declares the LORD, *plans to prosper you and not to harm you, plans to give you hope and a future."* God's plans for you may look radically different from where you find yourself now but remember, He created you to be better than the "you" you find yourself to be right now. Jeremiah tells us God has had great things planned in each of our lives from the very beginning. His works agree exactly with His thoughts; He does all according to the counsel of His will. *God's will for us is in favor of us, and not against us.* He will bless us to see the end of our troubles, the end of our sadness, and the end of the evil brought against us. His plans give us hope and a future. God wants us to be happy and prosperous; this is His will. III John 2 reads, *"Beloved, I wish above all things that thou mayest prosper and be in health, even as thy soul prospereth."* God wants us to have prosperity of the soul as well as prosperity of the body. Prosperity speaks to a state of well being brought about through our relationship with Him. Anything that leads you away from that relationship, plan and desire of God concerning you defiles you and dishonors Him.

We were created to honor Him, to worship Him, to praise Him, and to glorify who He is. In the uniqueness of each individual is the unchanging call upon God's creation to recognize Him in all of His deity. We have to recognize Him in that which He has specifically called us to. We all have a calling. It is incumbent upon us to hear God so He can make that calling known unto us. Where you are now may not be a place you can hear all of what God is trying to say to you. He made you better than who you are now. And you, through the help of God, have to find the "you" He created you to be. Esther found herself as queen divinely positioned to save her people. Moses was destined to deliver his people out of bondage. Nehemiah was called to go back to Jerusalem and rebuild the wall. Abraham was birthed to father a nation. John the Baptist was called to be the forerunner of Christ. David was called to reign over the chosen people. Solomon was called to build the temple. Peter was called to start the New Testament church. Paul was called to evangelize the world. And, God has called you too. Your calling may be to stop the perpetuation of abuse in your family. It may be to raise a family free of physical, mental, and emotional ills. It may be your charge in life to secure a generation that will go on to be godly teachers, lawyers, mathematicians, architects, astronauts, senators, concert pianist, and so much more. Whatever their occupation or status in life, they will be God-centered vessels, all the more ready to be instruments of God because you answered His call.

Think it not strange, that with all the greatness that lies in you, Satan would not do all he could to keep you from finding the true you in Christ. He will not only use, but he will orchestrate the hardness in family life to make you bitter, angry, and deaf to the calling of our God. When God sat in eternity past and looked through the portals of time, He saw the people of this millennium. He saw the hearts of the people, the conditions of society, the drifting away of the saints, and the alienation of daily living for Him. He saw drug addiction, violence, sickness, sexual perversion, divided families, hatred among races, witchcraft (in and out of the church), sin and division within the Body of Christ, war and unspeakable acts of crime against the innocent. He saw the need and He created you, and through your calling He predestined you to the Kingdom for such a time as this.

He made you better than this and He has the final say!

WriteHouse is a Full Service Publishing Company:
We make YOUR goal to publish DOABLE.

www.writehousepublishing.com

202.714.7724

www.ingramcontent.com/pod-product-compliance
Lightning Source LLC
Chambersburg PA
CBHW060555100426
42742CB00013B/2573